Love, Always

KK Foster

Presentation by *BookLeaf Publishing*

Web: www.bookleafpub.com

E-mail: info@bookleafpub.com

ISBN: 9789357213912

First edition 2022

To all those who love me unconditionally: it is because of your love, support, and faith in me, that I continue to become all that I am meant to be and who I am meant to be, authentically. I am so grateful. I love you more.

I AM

I have this voice
these eyes, this heart
I am a light, a truth
my own North Star
I am made of colors
some still unknown
there's so much magic in discovering
all that makes me whole
I AM creating my world
I AM the love I deserve
I AM creating my world
I AM LOVE, LOVE, LOVE
I AM creating my world
I AM the love I deserve
I AM creating my world
I AM LOVE, LOVE, LOVE

All That You Are

you are an ocean of stars
with a passionate heart
I wish you could see
all that you are
you're the rhythm of kindness
a safe space to fear less
your love is a music
a symphony to breathe in
you are enough
all that you are
you are enough
you are love, you are loved

All Is Well

I am valuable
I am here for a reason
all is well, all is well
even when I question myself
yes, all is well
as I learn to love myself
cause some days it's harder
to trust in the process
release and surrender
moment to moment
but I'm here with this heart
each beat, like my compass
I need to believe in myself
and let love flow
all is well

Keep Showing Up

keep showing up
keep showing up as you are
let every breath
radiate the love in your heart
keep taking the steps
keep creating your path
let the Earth ground you
as your energy carries you forward

Your Song

5

your heart is strong
it beats in love
and if you listen close
you'll hear your song
you are whole
as long as the rivers run
through every moment
you become your home
so hold on
don't give up
your light is alive
and you are enough

I Am My Home

I am my home
I am where I belong
I am rising above
I am letting go
and holding on
I am finding my way through love
I am my home
I am finding my way through love

Connecting with Creativity

the journey is ours
a circle of growth, an infinity of flow
where we create and we love
with our hearts and our souls
the connections find their reflections
within the vibrations
of the energies we hold
and we are made of stardust
with light that embraces the shadows
each breath, our air
inspiration for the lungs
so that we must allow ourselves the space
to be the spark, the fire, the sun
for we are music and we are art
words on pages and those in thought
with every step, gratitude fills us up
this Earth, that we are a part of
and our love is loud, colorful and proud
and with all our senses, we are powerful waves
wherever we go, we can create positive change
so let us dance and sing and simply be
let us learn and heal and live authentically
let us find ourselves and follow our dreams
with joy and laughter, and a touch of
vulnerability

with hope alongside love, I believe
we can be and do anything
letting the circle swirl on day to day
in the starts and stops and the inbetweens
for the Universe has our backs
all is well in perfect divine timing
so trust, we are who we choose to be
it is all possible
connecting with creativity

Keep Going

keep showing up
keep showing up as you are
let every breath
radiate the love in your heart
keep taking the steps
keep creating your path
let the Earth ground you
as your energy carries you forward

Love Lives

I'm learning more about who I am
through walls and scars to happiness
I let the sunlight sink into my skin
as I create myself in the moments
even when I stumble, even if I fall
every feeling, I've felt them all
still there's hope, alive in my heart
and with every breath, I'm grateful
cause love lives in every little thing
love is music the soul needs

We Are Worth It

I listen to the sun speaking
hear the waves singing songs of what could be
and there's hope in my veins
I'm here, and I believe
that if we rise with love, give all we've got
remind our hearts, we are worth it all
we can be the good vibes
we can be the rhythm and the starlight
to create the change in our lives
we are where the love resides

You're Loved

you're healing, take your time
the feelings, can hold on tight
keep breathing, you'll be alright
you're love, you're loved
and I, am on, your side
I am on your side
you're loved, you're loved
and I, am on, your side
I am on your side

Let Love, Be Your Medicine

let love, hold your hand
let love, help you, breathe it in
let love, have another chance
let love, help you feel again

let love, play your melody
let love, bring you peace
let love, heal your grief
let love, be you and me

let love, be your inspiration
let love, grow in between the moments
let love, be your medicine
let love, in again

let love, be your medicine
let love, in again

We Are Here

we are here, to grow
we are here, to hope
we are here, to love
we are here, each of us
we are here, to feel
we are here, to create
we are here, to love
and to know, we're enough
we are here, to be
the change we want to see
we are here, to love
so hold on
we are here, to love
so don't, give up

Love You

you are not alone
you are a light in this world
whether you're falling down
trying to find a way out
I promise, that you've got this
you can whisper, you can yell
you can second guess yourself
but you are stronger than you know
you are irreplaceable
and the story of your heart
is one you deserve to tell
I hope you love you
deep down to your soul
I want you to love you
cause you are worthy of it all

You Are Worthy

you are music
you are art
you are shade under branches of trees
you are collections of shooting stars
you are rainbows after storms
you are sunshine with a breeze
you are laughter and the rush
from what a kiss and holding hands can bring
I know, you don't always believe what you see
when you look in the mirror
but I'm asking you to trust me
take a breath, write it down, and speak
say I love you to yourself
that you matter, you are enough,
you are worthy
and repeat it as often as you need

Whole

I am me, a universe of possibilities
heart beating, let me breathe
I'm so much more than a binary
I'm collections, reflections
lessons learned
I am the rhythm, the beat,
the music, the meaning in the words
I'm a rainbow of all the colors
light, and darkness, combined
I am fear, hurt, happiness, and hope
I am a calming mantra and the butterflies
I feel beneath what just the eyes can see
I'm the bridge yet following my flow
I'm love that sinks in deep
I resonate in the soul
I'm inspired and inspiring
I believe in the fluidity of growth
I am healing, I am becoming
all that I am that makes me whole

I Am Love and I Am Enough

the mind and the heart
our thoughts and feelings
making up who we are
with each dream, believing
and as life goes on
we grow and we're changing
let us honor the call
if ever we need healing
authentic light
shining through our seams
for we are love
and we deserve to be seen
sometimes, we must say to ourselves
"hold on, deeps breaths now
I am worthy
I am love
I am love
and I am enough"

Your Story Is Yours

I feel you, in my bones
deep down, to my soul
you glow, like the stars are your own
and in every breath, it's love
you are more than the eyes can see
put your hand on heart
you are worthy
deep breath, just breathe
your story is yours for creating

No One Like You

you're perfect just as you are
with a strength of water and light of the stars
I know you don't always (see it or) believe it
but I'll remind you, show you
be there, beside you
cause there's no one else in this world
who has a heart like yours

One Step At A Time

I am growing, becoming
into all the me I hope to be
I am breathing, believing
in all the love meant for me
so here I am, I am going
one step at a time
heartbeat to heartbeat
trusting what I feel in my energy
letting love guide me

Trusting My Path

I walk along the river's edge
the sound of the water
helps calm the thoughts in my head
my eyes catch the way the sun reflects
a distraction, of nature's magic
a quiet reminder to take a deep breath
I've got to let go, surrender
trusting in my path ahead
hold on, remember
I am loved, I am worthy of
all my heart's desiring